Above Life's Turmoil

James Allen

DIAMOND BOOKS

www.diamondbooks.in

Publisher	:	**Diamond Pocket Books (P) Ltd.** X-30, Okhla Industrial Area, Phase-II New Delhi-110020
Phone	:	011-40712200
E-mail	:	wecare@diamondbooks.in
Website	:	www.diamondbooks.in
Edition	:	2024

Above Life's Turmoil
By - *James Allen*

About the Author

James Allen (1864–1912) was a British philosophical writer known primarily for his work on self-help and self-improvement. Also renowned for his influential works on personal development, character building, and the power of thought in shaping one's destiny. Allen is considered a pioneer in the realm of motivational and spiritual literature, offering timeless wisdom that continues to inspire readers around the world.

James Allen's writing is characterized by its simplicity, clarity, and profound insight. His works are often written in a meditative, almost poetic style, designed to provoke deep reflection. He believed that thoughts are the foundation of personal reality, a theme he explored extensively in his books. Allen's language is calm and instructive, focusing on moral and ethical improvement rather than intellectual complexity. His prose often conveys an underlying sense of compassion and earnestness, emphasizing that spiritual and material well-being are achievable through inner transformation.

Allen's works are deeply influenced by New Thought philosophy, emphasizing the law of attraction and the idea that our thoughts manifest in the physical world. His approach is direct, making complex spiritual ideas accessible. His sentences are concise, often designed to be memorable aphorisms, and his books contain practical advice on how to cultivate virtues such as patience, kindness, and diligence.

He stresses universal truths and the importance of self-discipline, mindfulness, and a strong moral character. His writing encourages self-examination, urging readers to take responsibility for their thoughts, actions, and ultimate destiny.

Allen's most famous book is *As a Man Thinketh* (1903), a work that encapsulates his core philosophy: that thoughts shape our reality. It remains a classic in the self-help genre, still widely read today for its timeless message about the transformative power of thought.

James Allen authored numerous books during his lifetime, focusing on self-help, spiritual development, and the power of thought. Here is a list of all the known books authored by him:

1. *From Poverty to Power* (1901)
2. *All These Things Added* (1903)
3. *Byways of Blessedness* (1904)
4. *Out from the Heart* (1904)
5. *The Life Triumphant* (1908)
6. *The Mastery of Destiny* (1909)
7. *The Way of Peace* (1907)
8. *The Path of Prosperity* (1907)
9. *The Heavenly Life* (1904)
10. *Morning and Evening Thoughts* (1909)
11. *Man: King of Mind, Body and Circumstance* (1909)
12. *Above Life's Turmoil* (1910)
13. *Eight Pillars of Prosperity* (1911)
14. *Foundation Stones to Happiness and Success* (1913, posthumous)
15. *The Shining Gateway* (1915, posthumous)
16. *Men and Systems* (1914, posthumous)
17. *Poems of Peace* (1913, posthumous)
18. *James Allen's Book of Meditations for Every Day in the Year* (1913, posthumous)
19. *Light on Life's Difficulties* (1912)
20. *The Divine Companion* (1919, posthumous)

These books emphasize the importance of thought, ethical living, and self-responsibility, forming a rich body of work in the self-improvement genre.

Preface

"Learn to master your thoughts and emotions to navigate life's challenges."

"Above Life's Turmoil" by James Allen is a collection of short essays that focus on how individuals can transcend the difficulties, challenges, and distractions of everyday life by cultivating inner strength, self-discipline, and moral integrity. The book is built on the premise that external circumstances do not define one's peace and happiness; rather, it is one's mental and emotional responses that shape their life experience.

Allen asserts that true serenity and contentment can only be achieved by mastering one's thoughts and emotions. He emphasizes the importance of personal responsibility, encouraging readers to refrain from blaming external factors for their suffering. According to Allen, the key to rising above life's turmoil lies in inner transformation—by controlling negative thoughts and aligning oneself with virtue and truth, individuals can elevate themselves beyond the stress and chaos of the world.

Throughout the book, Allen explores various themes such as patience, self-control, humility, and the power of thought. The central theme of the book is that true peace and success are achieved not through material wealth or external conditions, but through mental discipline and moral integrity. Allen asserts that those who learn to govern their thoughts, maintain their principles, and stay focused on higher ideals can rise "above life's turmoil."

One should read "Above Life's Turmoil" by James Allen for its timeless wisdom on achieving inner peace amidst life's challenges. The book teaches how to rise above stress, distractions, and hardships by mastering one's thoughts, cultivating virtues like patience and self-discipline, and aligning with higher moral principles. It offers practical guidance for personal growth, emphasizing that true happiness and success come from within, and not external circumstances. For those seeking mental clarity, emotional balance, and spiritual fulfillment, Allen's insights provide a path to living a calm, purpose-driven life.

Contents

Foreword

We cannot alter external things, nor shape other people to our liking, nor mould the world to our wishes but we can alter internal things,-our desires, passions, thoughts,-we can shape our liking to other people, and we can mould the inner world of our own mind in accordance with wisdom, and so reconcile it to the outer world if men and things. The turmoil of the world we cannot avoid, but the disturbances of mind we can overcome. The duties and difficulties of life claim our attention, but we can rise above all anxiety concerning them. Surrounded by noise, we can yet have a quiet mind; involved in responsibilities, the heart can be at rest; in the midst of strife, we can know the abiding peace. The twenty pieces which comprise this book, unrelated as some of them are in the letter, will be found to be harmonious in the spirit, in that they point the reader towards those heights of self-knowledge and self-conquest which, rising above the turbulance of the world, lift their peaks where the Heavenly Silence reigns.

James Allen

True Happiness

To maintain an unchangeable sweetness of disposition, to think only thoughts that are pure and gentle, and to be happy under all circumstances,- such blessed conditions and such beauty of character and life should be the aim of all, and particularly so of those who wish to lessen the misery of the world. If anyone has failed to lift himself above ungentleness, impurity, and unhappiness, he is greatly deluded if he imagines he can make the world happier by the propagation of any theory or theology. He who is daily living in harshness, impurity, or unhappiness is day by day adding to the sum of the world's misery; whereas he who continually lives in goodwill, and does not depart from happiness, is day by day increasing the sum of the world's happiness, and this independently of any religious beliefs which these may or may not hold.

He who has not learned how to be gentle, or giving, loving and happy, has learned very little, great though his book-learning and profound his acquaintance which the letter of Scripture may be, for it is in the process of becoming gentle, pure, and happy that the deep, real and enduring lessons of life are learned. Unbroken sweetness of conduct in the face of all outward antagonism is the infallible indication of a self-conquered soul, the witness of wisdom, and the proof of the possession of Truth.

A sweet and happy soul is the ripened fruit of experience and wisdom, and it sheds abroad the invisible yet powerful aroma of its influence, gladdening the hearts of others, and purifying the world. And all who will, and who have not yet commenced, may begin this day, if they will so resolve, to live sweetly and happily, as becomes the dignity of a true manhood or womanhood. Do not say that your surroundings are against you. A man's surroundings are never against him; they are there to aid him, and all those outward occurrences over which you lose sweetness and peace of mind are the very conditions necessary to your development, and it is only by meeting and overcoming them that you can learn, and grow, and ripen. The fault is in yourself.

Pure happiness is the rightful and healthy condition of the soul, and all may possess it if they will live purely and unselfish.

> "Have goodwill
> To all that lives, letting unkindness die,
> And greed and wrath, so that your lives be made
> Like soft airs passing by."

Is this too difficult for you? Then unrest and unhappiness will continue to dwell with you. Your belief and aspiration and resolve are all that are necessary to make it easy, to render it in the near future a thing accomplished, a blessed state realised.

Despondency, irritability, anxiety and complaining, condemning and grumbling-all these are thought-cankers, mind-diseases; they are the indications of a wrong mental condition, and those who suffer therefrom would do well to remedy their thinking and conduct. It is true there is much sin and misery in the world, so that all our love and compassion are needed, but our misery is not needed-there is already too much of that. No, it is our cheerfulness and happiness that are needed for there is too little of that. We can give nothing better to the world than beauty of life and character; without this, all other things are vain; this is pre-eminently excellent; it is enduring, real, and not to be overthrown, and it includes all joy and blessedness.

Cease to dwell pessimistically upon the wrongs around you; dwell no more in complaints about, and revolt against, the evil in others, and commence to live free from all wrong and evil yourself. Peace of mind, pure religion, and true reform lie this way. If you would have others true, be true; if you would have the world emancipated from misery and sin, emancipate yourself; if you would have your home and your surroundings happy, be happy. You can transform everything around you if you will transform yourself.

"Don't bewail and bemoan.....

Don't waste yourself in rejection, nor bark against the bad,

but chant the beauties of the good." _

And this you will naturally and spontaneously do as you realise the good in yourself.

The Immortal Man

Immortality is here and now, and is not a speculative something beyond the grave. It is a lucid state of consciousness in which the sensations of the body, the varying and unrestful states of mind, and the circumstances and events of life are seen to be of a fleeting and therefore of an illusory character.

Immortality does not belong to time, and will never be found in time; it belongs to Eternity; and just as time is here and now, so is Eternity here and now, and a man may find that Eternity and establish in it, if he will overcome the self that derives its life from the unsatisfying and perishable things of time.

Whilst a man remains immersed in sensation, desire, and the passing events of his day-by-day existence, and regards those sensations, desires, and passing events as of the essence of himself, he can have no knowledge of immortality. The thing which such a man desires, and which he mistakes for immortality, is persistence; that is, a continous succession of sensations and events in time. Living in, loving and clinging to, the things which stimulate and minister to his immediate gratification, and realising no state of consciousness above and independent of this, he thirsts for its continuance, and strives to banish the thought that he will at last have to part from those earthly luxuries and delights to which he has become enslaved, and which he regards as being inseparable from himself.

Persistence is the antithesis of immortality; and to be absorbed in it is spiritual death. Its very nature is change, impermanence. It is a continual living and dying.

The death of the body can never bestow upon a man immortality. Spirits are not different from men, and live their little feverish life of broken consciousness, and are still immersed in change and mortality. The mortal man, he who thirsts for the persistence of his pleasure-loving personality is still mortal after death, and only lives another life with a beginning and an end without memory of the past, or knowledge of the future.

The immortal man is he who has detached himself from the things of time by having ascended into that state of consciousness which is fixed and unvariable, and is not affected by passing events and sensations. Human life consists of an evermoving procession of events, and in this procession the mortal man is immersed, and he is carried along with it; and being so carried along, he has no knowledge of what is behind and before him. The immortal man is he who has stepped out of this procession, and he stands by unmoved and watches it; and from his fixed place he sees both the before, the behind and the middle of the moving thing called life. No longer identifying himself with the sensations and fluctuations of the personality, or with the outward changes which make up the life in time, he has become the passionless spectator of his own destiny and of the destinies of the men and nations.

The mortal man, also, is one who is caught in a dream, and he neither knows that he was formerly awake, nor that he will wake again; he is a dreamer without knowledge, nothing more. The immortal man is as one who has awakened out of his dream, and he knows that his dream was not an enduring reality, but a passing illusion. He is a man with knowledge, the knowledge of both states-that of persistence, and that of immortality,- and is in full possession of himself.

The mortal man lives in the time or world state of consciousness which begins and ends; the immortal man lives in the cosmic or heaven state of consciousness, in which there is neither beginning nor end, but an eternal now. Such a man remains poised and steadfast under all changes, and the death of his body will not in any way interrupt the eternal consciousness in which he abides. Of such a one it is said, "He shall not taste of death", because he has stepped out of the stream of mortality, and established himself in the abode of Truth. Bodies, personalities, nations, and worlds pass away, but Truth remains, and its glory is undimmed by time. The immortal man, then, is he who has conquered himself; who no longer identifies himself with the self-seeking forces of the personality, but who has trained himself to direct those forces with the hand of a master, and so has brought them into harmony with the causal energy and source of all things.

The fret and fever of life has ceased, doubt and fear are cast out, and death is not for him who has realised the fadeless splendour of that life of Truth by adjusting heart and mind to the eternal and unchangeable verities.

The Overcoming of Self

Many people have very confused and erroneous ideas concerning the terms "the overcoming of self", "the eradication of desire", and "the annihilation of the personality." Some (particularly the intellectual who are prone to theories) regard it as a metaphysical theory altogether apart from life and conduct; while others conclude that it is the crushing out of all life, energy and action, and the attempt to idealise stagnation and death. These errors and confusions, arising as they do in the minds of individuals, can only be removed by the individuals themselves; but perhaps it may make their removal a little less difficult (for those who are seeking Truth) by presenting the matter in another way.

The doctrine of the overcoming or annihilation of self is simplicity itself; indeed, so simple, practical, and close at hand is it that a child of five, whose mind has not yet become clouded with theories, theological schemes and speculative philosophies, would be far more likely to comprehend it than many older people who have lost their hold upon simple and beautiful truths by the adoption of complicated theories.

The annihilation of self consists in weeding out and destroying all those elements in the soul which lead to division, strife, suffering, disease and sorrow. It does not mean the destruction of any good and beautiful and peace-producing quality. For instance, when a man is tempted to irritability or anger, and by a great effort overcomes the selfish tendency, casts it from him, and acts from the spirit of patience and love, in that moment of self-conquest he practises the annihilation of self. Every noble man practises it in part, though he may deny it in his words, and he who carries out this practice to its completion, eradicating every selfish tendency until only the divinely beautiful qualities remain, he is said to have annihilated the personality (all the personal elements) and to have arrived at Truth.

The self which is to be annihilated is composed of the following ten worthless and sorrow-producing elements:

Compassion

Love

These comprise the Body of Truth, and to live entirely in them is to be a doer and knower of the Truth, is to be an embodiment of Truth. The combination of the ten elements is called Self or the Personality; the combination of the ten qualities produces what is called Truth; the Impersonal; the abiding, real and immortal Man.

It will thus be seen that it is not the destruction of any noble, true, and enduring quality that is taught, but only the destruction of those things that are ignoble, false and evanescent. Neither is this overcoming of self the deprivation of gladness, happiness and joy, but rather is it the constant possession of these things by living in the joy-begetting qualities. It is the abandonment of the lust for enjoyment, but not of enjoyment itself; the destruction of the thirst for pleasure, but not of pleasure itself; the annihilation of the selfish longing for love, and power, and possessions themselves. It is the preservation of all those things which draw and bind men together in unity and concord, and, far from idealising stagnation and death, urges men to the practice of those qualities which lead to the highest, noblest, most effective, and enduring action. He whose actions proceed from some or all of the ten elements wastes his energies upon negations, and does not preserve his soul; but he whose actions proceed from some or all of the ten qualities, he truly and wisely acts and so preserves his soul.

He who lives largely in the ten earthly elements, and who is blind and deaf to the spiritual verities, will find no attraction in the doctrine of self-surrender, for it will appear to him as the complete extinction of his being; but he who is endeavouring to live in the ten heavenly qualities will see the glory and beauty of the doctrine, and will know it as the foundation of Life Eternal. He will also see that when men apprehend and practise it, industry, commerce, government, and every worldly activity will be purified; and action, purpose and intelligence, instead of being destroyed, will be intensified and enlarged, but freed from strife and pain.

Wheresoever these are, there Brotherhood is active. In whatsoever heart these qualities are dominant, there Brotherhood is an established reality, for they are, in their very nature, unselfish and are filled with the revealing Light of Truth. There is no darkness in them, and where they are, so powerful is their light, that the dark tendencies cannot remain, but are dissolved and dissipated.

Out of these four qualities proceed all those angelic actions and conditions which make for unity and bring gladness to the heart of man and to the world.

From the spirit of Humility proceed meekness and peacefulness; from self-surrender come patience, wisdom, and true judgment; from Love spring kindness, joy, and harmony; and from Compassion proceed gentleness and forgiveness.

He who has brought himself into harmony with these four qualities is divinely enlightened; he sees whence the actions of men proceed and whither they tend, and therefore can no longer live in the exercise of the dark tendencies. He has realised Brotherhood in its completion as freedom from malice; from envy, from bitterness, from contention, from condemnation. All men are his brothers, those who live in the dark tendencies, as well as those who live in the enlightened qualities, for he knows that when they have perceived the glory and beauty of the Light of Truth, the dark tendencies will be dispelled from their minds. He has but one attitude of mind towards all, that of goodwill.

Of the four dark tendencies are born ill-will and strife; of the four divine qualities are born goodwill and peace.

Living in the four tendencies a man is a strife-producer. Living in the four qualities a man is a peace-maker.

Involved in the darkness of the selfish tendencies, men believe that they can fight for peace, kill to make alive, slay injury by injuring, restore love by hatred, unity by contention, kindness by cruelty, and establish brotherhood by erecting their own opinions (which they themselves will, in the course of time, abandon as worthless) as objects of universal adoration.

The wished-for Temple of Brotherhood will be erected in the world when its four foundation stones of Humility, Self-surrender, Love, and Compassion are firmly laid in the hearts of men, for Brotherhood consists, first of all, in the abandonment of self by the individual, and its after-effects is unity between man and man.

Theories and schemes for propagating Brotherhood are many, but Brotherhood itself is one and unchangeable and consists in the complete cessation from egotism and strife, and in practising goodwill and peace; for Brotherhood is a practice and not a theory. Self-surrender and Goodwill are its guardian angels, and peace is its habitation.

Where two are determined to maintain an opposing opinion, the clinging to self and ill-will are there, and Brotherhood is absent.

Where two are prepared to sympathise with each other, to see no evil in each other, to serve and not to attack each other; the Love of Truth and Goodwill are there, and Brotherhood is present.

All strifes, divisions, and wars inhere in the proud, unyielding self; all peace, unity, and concord inhere in the Principles which the yielding up of self reveals.

Brotherhood is only practised and known by him whose heart is at peace with all the world.

The Uses of Temptation

The soul, in its journey towards perfection, passes through three distinct stages. The first is the animal stage, in which the man is content to live, in the gratification of his senses, unawakened to the knowledge of sin, or of his divine inheritance, and altogether unconscious of the spiritual possibilities within himself.

The second is the dual stage, in which the mind is continually oscillating between its animal and divine tendencies having become awakened to the consciousness of both. It is during this stage that temptation plays its part in the progress of the soul. It is a stage of continual fighting, of falling and rising, of sinning and repenting, for the man, still loving, and reluctant to leave, the gratifications in which he has so long lived, yet also aspires to the purity and excellence of the spiritual state, and he is continually mortified by an undecided choice.

Urged on by the divine life within him, this stage becomes at last one of deep anguish and suffering, and then the soul is ushered into the third stage, that of knowledge , in which the man rises above both sin and temptation, and enters into peace.

Temptation, like contentment in sin, is not a lasting condition,as the majority of people suppose; it is a passing phase, an experience through which the soul must pass; but as to whether a man will pass through that condition in this present life, and realise holiness and heavenly rest here and now, will depend entirely upon the strength of his intellectual and spiritual exertions, and upon the intensity and ardour with which he searches for Truth.

Temptation, with all its attendant torments can be overcome here and now, but it can only be overcome by knowledge. It is a condition of darkness or of semi-darkness. The fully enlightened soul is proof against all temptation. When a man fully understands the source, nature, and meaning of temptation, in that hour he will conquer it, and will rest from his long travail; but whilst he remains in ignorance, attention to religious observances, and much praying and reading of Scripture will fail to bring him peace.

If a man goes out to conquer an enemy, knowing nothing of his enemy's strength, tactics, or place of ambush, he will not only ignominiously fail, but will speedily fall into the hands of the enemy. He who would overcome his enemy the tempter, must discover his stronghold and place of concealment, and must also find out the unguarded gates in his own fortress where his enemy effects so easy an entrance. This necessitates continual meditation, ceaseless watchfulness, and constant and rigid introspection which lays bare, before the spiritual eyes of the tempted one, the vain and selfish motives of his soul. This is the holy warfare of the saints; it is the fight upon which every soul enters when it awakens out of its long sleep of animal indulgence.

Men fail to conquer, and the fight is indefinitely prolonged, because they labour, almost universally, under two delusions: first, that all temptations come from without; and second, that they are tempted because of their goodness. Whilst a man is held in bondage by these two delusions, he will make no progress; when he has shaken them off, he will pass on rapidly from victory to victory, and will taste of spiritual joy and rest.

Two searching truths must take the place of these two delusions, and those truths are: first, that all temptation comes from within; and second, that a man is tempted because of the evil that is within him. The idea that God, a devil, evil spirits, or outward objects are the source of temptation must be dispelled.

The source and cause of all temptation is in the inward desire; that being purified or eliminated, outward objects and extraneous powers are utterly powerless to move the soul to sin or to temptation. The outward object is merely the occasion of the temptation, never the cause; this is in the desire of the one tempted. If the cause existed in the object, all men would be tempted alike, temptation could never be overcome, and men would be hopelessly doomed to endless torment; but seated, as it is, in his own desires, he has the remedy in his own hands, and can become victorious over all temptation by purifying those desires. A man is tempted because there are within him certain desires or states of mind which he has come to regard as unholy. Thes desires may lie asleep for a long time, and the man may think that he has got rid of them, when suddenly, on the presentation of an outward object, the sleeping desire wakes up and thirsts of immediate gratification; and this is the state of temptation.

The good in a man is never tempted. Goodness destroys temptation. It is the evil in a man that is aroused and tempted. The measure of a man's temptations is the exact register of his own unholiness. As a man purifies his heart, temptation ceases, for when a certain unlawful desire has been taken out of the heart, the object which formerly appealed to it can no longer do so, but becomes dead and powerless, for there is nothing left in the heart that can respond to it.The honest man cannot be tempted to steal, let the occasion be ever so opportune; the man of purified appeties cannot be tempted to gluttony and drunkenness, though the viands and wines be the most luscious; he of an enlightened understanding, whose mind is calm in the strength of inward virtue, can never be tempted to anger, irritability or revenge, and the wiles and charms of the wanton fall upon the purified heart as empty meaningless shadows.

Temptation shows a man just where he is sinful and ignorant, and is a means of urging him on to higher altitudes of knowledge and purity. Without temptation the soul cannot grow and become strong, there could be no wisdom, no real virtue; and though there would be lethargy and death, there could be no peace and no fulness of life. When temptation is understood and conquered, perfection is assured, and such perfection may bcome any man's who is willing to cast every selfish and impure desire by which he is possessed, into the sacrificial fire of knowledge. Let men, therefore, search diligently for Truth, realising that whilst they are subject to temptation, they have not comprehended Truth, and have much to learn.

Ye who are tempted know, then, that ye are tempted of yourselves. "For every man is tempted when he is drawn away of his own lusts," says the Apostle James. You are tempted because you are clinging to the animal within you and are unwilling to let go; because you are living in the false mortal self which is ever devoid of all true knowledge, knowing nothing, seeking nothing, but its own immediate gratification, ignorant of every Truth, and of every divine Principle. Clinging to that self, you continually suffer the pains of three separate torments; the torment of desire, the torment of repletion, and the torment of remorse.

> "So flameth Trishna, lust and thirst of things.
> Eager, ye cleave to shadows, dote on dreams;
> A false self in the midst ye plant, and make
> A World around which seems;
> Blind to the height beyond; deaf to the sound
> Of sweet airs breathed from far past Indra's sky;
> Dumb to the summons of the true life kept
> For him who false puts by,
> So grow the strifes and lusts which make earth's war,
> So grieve poor cheated hearts and flow salt tears;
> So wax the passions, envies, angers, hates;
> So years chase blood-stained years
> With wild red feet."

In that false self lies the germ of every suffering, the blight of every hope, the substance of every grief. When you are ready to give it up; when you are willing to have laid bare before you all its selfishness, impurity, and ignorance, and to confess its darkness to the uttermost, then will you enter upon the life of self-knowledge and self-mastery; you will become conscious of the god within you, of that divine nature which, seeking no gratification, abides in a region of perpetual joy and peace where suffering cannot come and where temptation can find no foothold. Establishing yourself, day by day, more and more firmly in that inward Divinity, the time will at last come when you will be able to say with Him whom millions worship, few understand and fewer still follow, - “The Prince of this world cometh and hath nothing in me.”

The Man of Integrity

There are times in the life of every man who takes his stand on high moral principles when his faith in, and knowledge of, those principles is tested to the uttermost, and the way in which he comes out of the fiery trial decides as to whether he has sufficient strength to live as a man of Truth, and join the company of the free, or shall still remain a slave and a hireling to the cruel taskmaster, Self.

Such times of trial generally assume the form of a temptation to do a wrong thing and continue in comfort and prosperity, or to stand by what is right and accept poverty and failure; and so powerful is the trial that, to the tempted one, it plainly appears on the face of things as though, if he chooses the wrong, his material success will be assured for the remainder of his life, but if he does what is right, he will be ruined for ever.

Frequently the man at once quails and gives way before this appalling prospect which the Path of Righteousness seems to hold out for him, but should he prove sufficiently strong to withstand this onslaught of temptation, then the inward seducer the spirit of self, assumes the grab of an Angel of Light, and whispers, "Think of your wife and children; think of those who are dependent upon you; will you bring them down to disgrace and starvation?"

Strong indeed and pure must be the man who can come triumphant out of such a trial, but he who does so, enters at once a higher realm of life, where his spiritual eyes are opened to see beautiful things; and then poverty and ruin which seemed inevitable do not come, but a more abiding success comes, and a peaceful heart and a quiet conscience. But he who fails does not obtain the promised prosperity, and his heart is restless and his conscience troubled.

The right-doer cannot ultimately fail, the wrong-doer cannot ultimately succeed, for

"Such is the Law which moves to Righteousness

Which none at last can turn aside or stay,"

and it is because justice is at the heart of things-because the Great Law is good-that the man of integrity is superior to fear, and failure, and poverty, and shame, and disgrace.As the poet further says of this Law:

"The heart of its Love, the end of it
Is peace and cosummation sweet-obey."

The man who fearing the loss of present pleasures or material comforts, denies the Truth within him, can be injured, and robbed, and degraded, and trampled upon, because he has first injured, robbed and degraded, and trampled upon his own nobler self; but the man of steadfast virtue, of unblemished integrity, cannot be subject to such conditions, because he has denied the craven self within him and has taken refuge in Truth. It is not the scourge and the chains which make a man a slave, but the fact that he is a slave.

Slander, Accusation, and malice cannot affect the righteous man, nor call from him any bitter response, nor does he need to go about to defend himself and prove his innocence. His innocence and integrity alone are a sufficient answer to all that hatred may attempt against him. Nor can he ever be subdued by the forces of darkness, having subdued all those forces within himself; but he turns all evil things to good account - out of darkness he brings light, out of hatred love, out of dishonour honour; and slanders, envies, and misrepresentations only serve to make more bright the jewel of Truth within him, and to glorify his high and holy destiny.

Let the man of integrity rejoice and be glad when he is severely tried; let him be thankful that he has been given an opportunity of proving his loyalty to the noble principles which he has espoused; and let him think: "Now is the hour of holy opportunity! Now is the day of triumph for Truth! Though I lose the whole world I will note desert the right!" So thinking, he will return good for evil, and will think compassionately of the wrong-doer.

The slanderer, the backbiter, and the wrong-doer may seem to succeed for a time, but the Law of Justice prevails; the man of integrity may seem to fail for a time, but he is invincible, and in none of the worlds, visible or invisible, can there be forged a weapon that shall prevail against him.

Discrimination

There is one quality which is pre-eminently necessary to spiritual development, the quality of discrimination.

A man's spiritual progress will be painfully slow and uncertain until there opens with him the eye of discrimination, for without this testing, proving, searching quality, he will but grope in the dark, will be unable to distinguish the real from the unreal, the shadow from the substance, and will so confuse the false with the true as to mistake the inward promptings of his animal nature for those of the spirit of Truth.

A blind man left in a strange place may go grope his way in darkness, but not without much confusion and many painful falls and bruisings. Without discrimination a man is mentally blind, and his life is a painful groping in darkness, a confusion in which vice and virtue are indistinguishable one from the other, where facts are confounded with truths; opinions with principles, and where ideas, events, men, and things appear to be out of all relation to each other.

A man's mind and life should be free from confusion. He should be prepared to meet every mental, material and spritual difficulty, and should not be inextricably caught (as many are) in the meshes of doubt, indecision and uncertainity when troubles and so-called misfortunes come along. He should be fortified against every emergency that can come against him; but such mental preparedness and strength cannot be attained in any degree without discrimination, and discrimination can only be developed by bringing into play and constantly exercising the analytical faculty.

Mind, like muscle, is developed by use, and the assiduous exercise of the mind in any given direction will develop, in that direction, mental capacity and power. The merely critical faculty is developed and strengthened by continuously comparing and analysing the ideas and opinions of others. But discrimination is something more and greater than criticism; it is a spiritual quality from which the cruelty and egotism which so frequently accompany criticism are eliminated, and by virtue of which a man sees things as they are, and not as he would like them to be.

Discrimination, being a spiritual quality, can only be developed by spiritual methods, namely, by questioning, examining, and analysing one's own ideas, opinions, and conduct. The critical, fault finding faculty must be withdrawn from its merciless application to the opinions and conduct of others, and must be applied, with undiminished severity, to oneself. A man must be prepared to question his every opinion, his every thought, and his every line of conduct, and rigorously and logically test them; only in this way can the discrimination which destroys confusion will be developed.

Before a man can enter upon such mental exercise, he must make himself of a teachable spirit. This does not mean that he must allow himself to be led by others; it means that he must be prepared to yield up any cherished thoughts to which he clings, if it will not bear the penetrating light of reason, if it shrivels up before the pure flames of searching aspirations. The man who says, "I am right!" and who refuses to question his position in order to discover whether he is right, will continue to follow the line of his passions and prejudices, and will not acquire discrimination. The man who humbly asks, "Am I right?" and then proceeds to test and prove his position by earnest thought and the love of Truth, will always be able to discover the true and to distinguish it from the false, and he will acquire the priceless possession of discrimination.

The man who is afraid to think searchingly upon his opinions, and to reason critically upon his position, will have to develop moral courage before he can acquire discrimination.

A man must be true to himself, fearless with himself, before he can perceive the Pure Principles of Truth, before he can receive the all-revealing Light of Truth.

The more Truth is inquired of, the brighter it shines; it cannot suffer under examination and analysis.

The more error is questioned, the darker it grows; it cannot survive the entrance of pure and searching thought.

To "prove all things" is to find the good and throw the evil.

He who reasons and meditates learns to discriminate; he who discriminates discovers the eternally True.

Confusion, suffering and spiritual darkness follow the thoughtless.

Harmony, blessedness and the Light of Truth attend upon the thoughtful.

Passion and prejudice are blind, and cannot discriminate: they are still crucifying the Christ and releasing Barabbas.

Belief, The Basis of Action

Belief is an important word in the teachings of the wise, and it figures prominently in all religions. According to Jesus, a certain kind of belief is necessary to salvation or regeneration, and Buddha definitely taught that right belief is the first and most essential step in the Way of Truth, as without right belief there cannot be right conduct, and he who has not learned how to rightly govern and conduct himself, has not yet comprehended the simplest rudiments of Truth.

Belief as laid down by the Great Teachers, is not belief in any particualr school, philosophy, or religion, but consists of an altitude of mind determining the whole course of one's life. Belief and conduct are, therefore inseparable, for the one determines the other.

Belief is the basis of all action, and, this being so, the belief which dominates the hearts or mind is shown in the life. Every man acts, thinks, lives in exact accordance with the belief which is rooted in his innermost being, and such is the mathematical nature of the laws which govern mind that it is absolutely impossible for anyone to believe in two opposing conditions at the same time. For instance, it is impossible to believe in justicc and injustice, hatred and love, peace and strife, self and truth. Every man believes in one or the other of these opposites, never in both, and the daily conduct of every man indicates the nature of his belief. The man who believes in justice, who regards it as an eternal and indestructible Principle, never boils over with righteous indignation, does not grow cynical and pessimistic over the inequalities of life, and remains calm and untroubled through all trials and difficulties. It is impossible for him to act otherwise, for he believes that justice reigns, and that, therefore, all that is called injustice is fleeting and illusory.

The man who is continually getting enraged over the injustice of his fellow men, who talks about himself being badly treated, or who mourns over the lack of justice in the world around him, shows by his conduct, his attitude of mind, that he believes in injustice. However he may protest to the contrary, in his inmost heart he believes that confusion and chaos are dominant in the universe, the result being that he dwells in misery and unrest, and his conduct is faulty.

Again, he who believes in love, in its stability and power, practises it under all circumstances, never deviates from it, and bestows it alike upon enemies as upon friends. He who slanders and condemns, who speaks disparagingly of others, or regards them with contempt, believes not in love, but hatred; all his actions prove it, even though with tongue or pen he may eulogise love.

The believer in peace is known by his peaceful conduct. It is impossible for him to engage in strife. If attacked he does not retaliate, for hc has seen the majesty of the angel of peace, and he can no longer pay homage to the demon of strife. The stirrer-up of strife, the lover of argument, he who rushes into self-defence upon any or every provocation, believes in strife, and will have naught to do with peace.

Further, he who believes in Truth renounces himself-that is, he refuses to centre his life in those passions, desires, and characteristics which crave only their own gratification, and by thus renouncing he becomes steadfastly fixed in Truth, and lives a wise, beautiful, and blameless life. The believer in self is known by his daily indulgences, gratifications, and vanities, and by the disappointments, sorrows, and mortifications which he continually suffers.

The believer in Truth does not suffer, for he has given up that self which is the cause of such suffering.

It will be seen by the foregoing that every man believes either in permanent and eternal Principles directing human life towards law and harmony, or in the negation of those Principles, with the resultant chaos in human affairs and in his own life.

Belief in the divine Principles of Justice, Compassion, Love, constitutes the right belief laid down by Buddha as being the basis of right conduct, and also the belief unto salvation as emphasised in the Christian Scriptures, for he who so believes cannot do otherwise than build his whole life upon these Principles, and so purifies his heart, and perfects his life.

Belief in the negation of this divine principle constitutes what is called in all religious unbelief and this unbelief is manifested as a sinful, troubled, and imperfect life.

Where there is Right Belief there is a blameless and perfect life; where there is false belief there is sin, there is sorrow, the mind and life are improperly governed, and there is affliction and unrest. "By their fruits ye shall know them."

There is much talk about, "belief in Jesus," but what does belief in jesus mean? It means belief in his words, in the Principles he enunciated-and lived, in his commandments and in his exemplary life of perfection. He who declares belief in Jesus, and yet is all the time living in his lusts and indulgences, or in the spirit of hatred and condemnation, is self deceived. He believes not in Jesus. He believes in his own animal self. As a faithful servant delights in carrying out the commands of his master, so he who believes in Jesus carries out his commandments, and so is saved from sin. The supreme test of belief in Jesus is this: Do I keep his commandments? And this test is applied by St.John himself in the following words: "He that saith. I know him (Jesus), and keepeth not His Commandments, is a liar, and the truth is not in him. But whoso keepeth his word, in him verily is the word of God perfected."

It will be found after a rigid and impartial analysis, that belief lies at the root of all human conduct. Every thought, every act, every habit, is the direct outcome of a certain fixed belief, and one's conduct alters only as one's belief are modified. What we cling to, in that we believe; what we practise, in that we believe. When our belief in a thing ceases, we can no longer cling to or practise it; it falls away from us as a garment out-worn. Men cling to their lusts, and lies, and vanities, because they believe in them, believe there is gain and happiness in them. When they transfer their belief to the divine qualities of purity and humility, those sins trouble them no more.

Men are saved from error by belief in the supremacy of Truth. They are saved from sin by belief in Holiness or Perfection. They are saved from evil by belief in Good, for every belief is manifested in the life. It is not necessary to inquire as to a man's theological belief, for that is of little or no account, for what can it avail a man to believe that Jesus died for him, or that Jesus is God, or that he is "justified by faith," if he continues to live in his lower, sinful nature? All that is necessary to ask is this: "How does a man live?" "How does he conduct himself under trying circumstances?" The answer to these questions will show whether a man believes in the power of evil or in the power of Good.

He who believes in the power of Good, lives a good, spiritual, or godly life, for Goodness is God, yea, verily is God Himself, and he will soon leave behind him all sins and sorrows who believes, with steadfast and unwavering faith, in the Supreme Good.

The Belief That Saves

It has been said that a man's whole life and character is the outcome of his belief, and also that his belief has nothing whatever to do with his life. Both statements are true. The confusion and contradiction of these two statements are only apparent, and are quickly dispelled when it is remembered that there are two entirely distinct kinds of beliefs, namely, Head-belief and Heart-belief .

Head, or intellectual belief, is not fundamental and causative, but it is superficial and consequent, and that it has no power in the moulding of a man's character, the most superficial observer may easily see. Take, for instance, half a dozen men from any creed. They not only hold the same theological belief, but confess the same articles of faith in every particular, and yet their characters are vastly different. One will be just as noble as another is ignoble; one will be mild and gentle, another coarse and irascible; one will be honest, another dishonest; one will indulge certain habits which another will rigidly abjure, and so on, plainly indicating that theological belief is not an influential factor in a man's life.

A man's theological belief is merely his intellectual opinion or view of the universe. God, The Bible, etc., and behind and underneath this head-belief there lies, deeply rooted in his innermost being, the hidden, silent, secret belief of his heart, and it is this belief which moulds and makes his whole life. It is this which makes those six men who, whilst holding the same theology, are yet so vastly at variance in their deeds-they differ in the vital belief of the heart.

What, then, is this heart-belief?

It is that which a man loves and clings to and fosters in his soul; for he thus loves and clings to and fosters in his heart, because he believes in them, and believing in them and loving them, he practises them; thus is his life the effect of his belief , but it has no relation to the particular creed which comprises his intellectual belief. One man clings to impure and immoral things because he believes in them; another does not cling to them because he has ceased to believe in them. A man cannot cling to anything unless he believes in it; belief always precedes action, therefore a man's deeds and life are the fruits of his belief.

The Priest and the Levite who passed by the injured and helpless man, held, no doubt, very strongly to the theological doctrines of their fathers-that was their intellectual belief,- but in their hearts they did not believe in mercy, and so lived and acted accordingly. The good Samaritan may or may not have had any theological beliefs nor was it necessary that he should have; but in his heart he believed in mercy, and acted accordingly.

Strictly speaking, there are only two beliefs which vitally affect the life, and they are, belief in good and belief in evil.

He who believes in all those things that are good, will love them, and live in them; he who believes in those things that are impure and selfish, will love them, and cling to them. The tree is known by its fruits.

A man's beliefs about God, Jesus, and the Bible are one thing; his life, as bound up in his actions, is another; therefore a man's theological belief is of no consequence; but the thoughts which he harbours, his attitude of mind towards others, and his actions, these, and these only, determine and demonstrate whether the belief of a man's heart is fixed in the false or true.

Thought And Action

As the fruit to the tree and the water to the spring, so is action to thought. It does not come into manifestation suddenly and without a cause. It is the result of a long and silent growth; the end of a hidden process which has long been gathering force. The fruit of the tree and the water gushing from the rock are both the effect of a combination of natural processes in air and earth which have long worked together in secret to produce the phenomenon; and the beautiful acts of enlightenment and the dark deeds of sin are both the ripened effects of trains of thought which have long been harboured in the mind.

The sudden falling, when greatly tempted, into some grievous sin by one who was believed, and who probably believed himself, to stand firm, is seen neither to be a sudden nor a causeless thing when the hidden process of thought which led up to it are revealed. The falling was merely the end, the outworking, the finished result of what commenced in the mind probably years before. The man had allowed a wrong thought to enter his mind; and a second and a third time he had welcomed it, and allowed it to nestle in his heart. Gradually he became accustomed to it, and cherished, and fondled, and tended it; and so it grew, until at last it attained such strength and force that it attracted to itself the opportunity which enabled it to burst forth and ripen into act. As falls the stately building whose foundations have been gradually undermined by the action of water, so at last falls the strong man who allows corrupt thoughts to creep into his mind and secretly undermine his character.

When it is seen that all sin and temptation are the natural outcome of the thoughts of the individual, the way to overcome sin and temptation becomes plain, and its achievement a near possibility, and, sooner or later, a certain reality; for if a man will admit, cherish, and brood upon thoughts that are pure and good, those thoughts, just as surely as the impure, will grow and gather force, and will at last attract to themselves the opportunities which will enable them to ripen into act.

"There is nothing hidden that shall not be revealed," and every thought that is harboured in the mind must, by virtue of the impelling force which is inherent in the universe, at last blossom into act good or bad according to its nature. The divine Teacher and the sensualist are both the product of their own thoughts, and have become what they are as the result of the seeds of thought which they have implanted, are allowed to fall, into the garden of the heart, and have afterwards watered, tended, and cultivated.

Let no man think he can, overcome sin and temptation by wrestling with opportunity; he can only overcome them by purifying his thoughts; and if he will, day by day, in the silence of his soul, and in the performance of his duties, strenuously overcome all erroneous inclination, and put in its place thoughts that are true and that will endure the light, opportunity to do evil will give place to opportunity for accomplishing good, for a man can only attarct that to him which is in harmony with his nature, and no temptation can gravitate to a man unless there is that in his heart which is capable of responding to it.

Guard well your thoughts, reader, for what you really are in your secret thoughts today, be it good or evil, you will, sooner or later, become in actual deed. He who unwearingly guards the portals of his mind against the intrusion of sinful thoughts, and occupies himself with loving thoughts, with pure, strong, and beautiful thoughts, will, when the season of their ripening comes, bringforth the fruits of gentle and holy deeds, and no temptation that can come against him shall find him unarmed or unprepared.

Your Mental Attitude

As a being of thought, your dominant mental attitude will determine your condition in life. It will also be the gauge of your knowledge and the measures of your attainment. The so-called limitations of your nature are the boundary lines of your thoughts; they are self-erected fences, and can be drawn to a narrower circle, extended to a wider, or be allowed to remain.

You are the thinker of your thoughts and as such you are the maker of yourself and condition. Thought is causal and creative, and appears in your character and life in the form of results. There are no accidents in your life. Both its harmonies and antagonisms are the responsive echoes of your thoughts. A man thinks, and his life appears.

If your dominant mental attitude is peaceable and lovable, bliss and blessedness will follow you; if it be resistant and hateful, trouble and distress will cloud your pathway. Out of ill-will will come grief and disaster; out of goodwill, healing and reparation.

You imagine your circumstances as being separate from yourself, but they are intimately related to your thought world. Nothing appears without an adequate cause. Everything that happens is just. Nothing is fated, everything is formed.

As you think, you travel; as you love, you attract. You are today where your thoughts have brought you; you will be tomorrow where your thoughts take you. You cannot escape the result of your thoughts, but you can endure and learn, can accept and be glad.

You will always come to the place where your love (your most abiding and intense thought) can receive its measure of gratification. If your love be base, you will come to a base place; if it be beautiful, you will come to a beautiful place.

You can alter your thoughts, and so alter your condition. Strive to perceive the vastness and grandeur of your responsibility. You are powerful, not powerless. You are as powerful to obey as you are to disobey; as strong to be pure as to be impure; as ready for wisdom as for ignorance. You can learn what you will, can remain as ignorant as you choose. If you love knowledge you will obtain it; if you love wisdom you will secure it; if you love purity you will realise it. All things await your acceptance, and you choose by the thoughts which you entertain.

A man remains ignorant because he loves ignorance, and chooses ignorant thoughts; a man becomes wise because he loves wisdom and chooses wise thoughts. No man is hindered by another; he is only hindered by himself. No man suffers because of another; he suffers only because of himself. By the noble Gateway of Pure Thought you can enter the highest Heaven; by the ignoble doorway of impure thought you can descend into the lowest hell.

Your mental attitude towards others will faithfully react upon yourself, and will manifest itself in every relation of your life. Every impure and selfish thought that you send out comes back to you in your circumstances in some form of suffering; every pure and unselfish thought returns to you in some form of blessedness. Your circumstances are effects of which the cause is inward and invisible. As the father-mother of your thoughts you are the maker of your state and condition. When you know yourself, you will perceive, that every event in your life is weighed in the faultless balance of equity. When you understand the law within your mind you will cease to regard yourself as the impotent and blind tool of circumstances, and will become the strong and seeing master.

Sowing And Reaping

Go into the fields and country lanes in the spring-time, and you will see farmers and gardeners busy sowing seeds in the newly prepared soil. If you were to ask any one of those gardeners or farmers what kind of produce he expected from the seed he was sowing, he would doubtless regard you as foolish, and would tell you that he does not "expect" at all, that it is a matter of common knowledge that his produce will be of the kind which he is sowing, and that he is sowing wheat, or barley, or turnips, as the case may be, in order to reproduce that particular kind.

Every fact and process in Nature contains a moral lesson for the wise man. There is no law in the world of Nature around us which is not to be found operating with the same mathematical certainty in the mind of man and in human life. All the parables of Jesus are illustrative of this truth, and are drawn from the simple facts of Nature. There is a process of seed-sowing in the mind and life a spiritual sowing which leads to a harvest according to the kind of seed sown. Thoughts, words, and acts are seeds sown, and, by the inviolable law of things, they produce after their kind.

The man who thinks hateful thoughts brings hatred upon himself. The man who thinks loving thoughts is loved. The man whose thoughts, words and acts are sincere, is surrounded by sincere friends; the insincere man is surrounded by insincere friends. The man who sows wrong thoughts and deeds, and prays that God will bless him, is in the position of a farmer who, having sown tares, asks God to bring forth for him a harvest of wheat.

> "That which ye sow, ye reap; see yonder fields
> The sesamum was sesamum, the corn
> Was corn; the silence and the darkness knew;
> So is a man's fate born."
> "He cometh reaper of the things he sowed."

He who would be blest, let him scatter blessings. He who would be happy, let him consider the happiness of others.

Then there is another side to this seed sowing. The farmer must scatter all his seed upon the land, and then leave it to the elements. Were he to covetously hoard his seed, he would lose both it and his produce, for his seed would perish. It perishes when he sows it, but in perishing it brings forth a great abundance. So in life, we get by giving; we grow rich by scattering. The man who says he is in possession of knowledge which he cannot give out because the world is incapable of receiving it, either does not possess such knowledge, or, if he does, will soon be deprived of it - if he is not already so deprived. To hoard is to lose; to exclusively retain is to be dispossessed.

Even the man who would increase his material wealth must be willing to part with (invest) what little capital he has, and then wait for the increase. So long as he retains his hold on his precious money, he will not only remain poor, but will be growing poorer everyday. He will, after all, lose the thing he loves, and will lose it without increase. But if he wisely lets it go; if, like the farmer, he scatters his seeds of gold, then he can faithfully wait for, and reasonably expect, the increase.

Men are asking God to give them peace and purity, and righteousness and blessedness, but are not obtaining these things; and why not? Because they are not practising them, not sowing them. I once heard a preacher pray very earnestly for forgiveness, and shortly afterwards, in the course of his sermon, he called upon his congregation to "show no mercy to the enemies of the church." Such self-delusion is pitiful, and men have yet to learn that the way to obtain peace and blessedness is to scatter peaceful and blessed thoughts, words, and deeds.

Men believe that they can sow the seeds of strife, impurity, and unbrotherliness, and then gather in a rich harvest of peace, purity and concord by merely asking for it. What more pathetic sight than to see an irritable and quarrelsome man praying for peace. Men reap that which they sow, and any man can reap all blessedness now and at once, if he will put aside selfishness, and sow broadcast the seeds of kindness, gentleness, and love.

If a man is troubled, perplexed, sorrowful, or unhappy, let him ask:

"What mental seeds have I been sowing?"

"What seeds am I sowing?"

"What have I done for others?"

"What is my attitude towards others?"

"What seeds of trouble and sorrow and unhappiness have I sown that I should thus reap these bitter weeds?"

Let him seek within and find, and having found, let him abandon all the seeds of self, and sow, henceforth, only the seeds of Truth.

Let him learn of the farmer the simple truths of wisdom.

The Reign Of Law

The little party gods have had their day. The arbitrary gods, creatures of human caprice and ignorance, are falling into disrepute. Men have quarrelled over and defended them until they have grown weary of the strife, and now, everywhere, they are relinquishing and breaking up these helpless idols of their long worship.

The god of revenge, hatred and jealousy, who gloats over the downfall of his enemies; the partial god who gratifies all our narrow and selfish desires; the god who saves only the creatures of his particular special creed; the god of exclusiveness and favouritism; such were the gods (miscalled by us God) of our soul's infancy, gods base and foolish as ourselves, the fabrications of our selfish self. And we relinquished our petty gods with bitter tears and misgivings, and broke our idols with bleeding hands. But in so doing we did not lose sight of God; nay we drew nearer to the great, silent Heart of Love. Destroying the idols of self, we began to comprehend somewhat of the Power which cannot be destroyed, and entered into a wider knowledge of the God of Love, of Peace, of Joy; the God in whom revenge and partiality cannot exist; the God of Light, from whose presence the darkness of fear and doubt and selfishness cannot choose but flee.

We have reached one of those epochs in the world's progress which witnesses the passing of the false gods; the gods of human selfishness and human illusion. The new-old revelation of one universal impersonal Truth has again dawned upon the world, and its searching light has carried consternation to the perishable gods who take shelter under the shadow of self.

Men have lost faith in a god who can be cajoled, who rules arbitrarily and capriciously, subverting the whole order of things to gratify the wishes of his worshippers, and are turning, with a new light in their eyes and a new joy in their hearts, to the God of Law.

And to Him they turn, not for personal happiness and gratification, but for knowledge, for understanding, for wisdom, for liberation from the bondage of self. And thus turning, they do not seek in vain, nor are they sent away empty and discomfited. They find within themselves the reign of Law, that every thought, every impulse, every act and word brings about a result in exact accordance with its own nature; that thoughts of love bring about beautiful and blissful conditions, that hateful thoughts bring about distorted and painful conditions, that thoughts and acts good and evil are weighed in the faultless balance of the Supreme Law, and receive their equal measure of blessedness on the one hand, and misery on the other. And thus finding they enter a new Path, the Path of Obedience to the Law. Entering that Path they no longer accuse, no longer doubt, no longer fret and despond, for they know that God is right, the universal laws are right, the cosmos is right, and that they themselves are wrong, if wrong there is, and that their salvation depends upon themselves, upon their own efforts, upon their personal acceptance of that which is good and deliberate rejection of that which is evil. No longer merely hearers, they become doers of the Word, and they acquire knowledge, they receive understanding, they grow in wisdom, and they enter into the glorious life of liberation from the bondage of self.

"The Law of the Lord is perfect, enlightening the eyes." Imperfection lies in man's ignorance, in man's blind folly. Perfection, which is knowledge of the Perfect Law, is ready for all who earnestly seek it; it belongs to the order of things; it is yours and mine now if we will only put self-seeking on one side, and adopt the life of self-obliteration.

The knowledge of Truth, with its unspeakable joy, its calmness and quiet strength, is not for those who persist in clinging to their "rights," defending their "interests," and fighting for their "opinions"; whose works are imbued with the personal "I," and who build upon the shifting sands of selfishness and egotism. It is for those who renounce these causes of strife, these sources of pain and sorrow; and they are, indeed, Children of Truth, disciples of the Master, worshippers of the most High.

The Children of Truth are in the world today; they are thinking, acting, writing, speaking; yea, even prophets are amongst us, and their influence is pervading the whole earth. An undercurrent of holy joy is gathering force in the world, so that men and women are moved with new aspirations and hopes, and even those who neither see nor hear, feel within themselves strange yearnings after a better and fuller life.

The Law reigns, and it reigns in men's hearts and lives; and they have come to understand the reign of Law who have sought out the Tabernacle of the true God by the fair pathway of unselfishness.

God does not alter for man, for this would mean that the perfect must become imperfect; man must alter for God, and this implies that the imperfect must become perfect. The Law cannot be broken for man, otherwise confusion would ensue; man must obey the Law; this is in accordance with harmony, order, justice.

There is no more painful bondage than to be at the mercy of one's inclinations; no greater liberty than utmost obedience to the Law of Being. And the Law is that the heart shall be purified, the mind regenerated, and the whole being brought in subjection to Love till self is dead and Love is all in all, for the reign of Law is the reign of Love. And Love waits for all , rejecting none. Love may be claimed and entered into now, for it is the heritage of all.

Ah, beautiful Truth! To know that now man may accept his divine heritage, and enter the Kingdom of Heaven!

Oh, pitiful error! To know that man rejects it because of love of self!

Obedience to the Law means the destruction of sin and self, and the realisation of unclouded joy and undying peace.

Clinging to one's selfish inclinations means the drawing about one's soul clouds of pain and sorrow which darken the light of Truth; the shutting out of oneself from all real blessedness; for "whatsoever a man sows that shall he also reap."

Verily the Law reigneth, and reigneth for ever, and Justice and Love are its eternal ministers.

The Supreme Justice

The material universe is maintained and preserved by the equilibrium of its forces.

The moral universe is sustained and protected by the perfect balance of its equivalents.

As in the physical world Nature abhors a vaccum, so in the spiritual world disharmony is annulled.

Underlying the disturbances and destructions of Nature, and behind the mutability of its forms, there abides the eternal and perfect mathematical symmetry; and at the heart of life, behind all its pain, uncertainty, and unrest, there abide the eternal harmony, the unbroken peace, and inviolable Justice.

Is there, then, no injustice in the universe? There is injustice, and there is not. It depends upon the kind of life and the state of consciousness from which a man looks out upon the world and judges. The man who lives in his passions sees injustice everywhere; the man who has overcome his passions, sees the operations of Justice in every department of human life. Injustice is the confused, feverish dream of passion, real enough to those who are dreaming it; Justice is the permanent reality in life, gloriously visible to those who have wakened out of the painful nightmare of self.

The Divine Order cannot be perceived until passion and self are transcended; the Faultless Justice cannot be apprehended until all sense of injury and wrong is consumed in the pure flames of all-embracing Love.

The man who thinks, "I have been slighted, I have been injured, I have been insulted, I have been treated unjustly," cannot know what Justice is; blinded by self, he cannot perceive the pure Principles of Truth, and brooding upon his wrongs, he lives in continual misery.

In the region of passion there is a ceaseless conflict of forces causing suffering to all who are involved in them. There is action and reaction, deed and consequence, cause and effect; and within and above all is the Divine Justice regulating the play of forces with the utmost mathematical accuracy, balancing cause and effect with the finest precision. But this Justice is not perceived - cannot be perceived - by those who are engaged in the conflict; before this can be done, the fierce warfare of passion must be left behind.

The world of passion is the abode of schisms, quarrellings, wars, law-suits, accusations, condemnations, impurities, weaknesses, follies, hatreds, revenges, and resentments. How can a man perceive Justice or understand Truth who is even partly involved in the fierce play of its blinding elements? As well expect a man caught in the flames of a burning building to sit down and reason out the cause of the fire.

In this realm of passion, men see injustice in the actions of others because, seeing only immediate appearances, they regard every act as standing by itself, undetached from cause and consequence. Having no knowledge of cause and effect in the moral sphere, men do not see the exacting and balancing process which is momentarily proceeding, nor do they ever regard their own actions as unjust, but only the actions of others. A boy beats a defenceless animal, then a man beats the defenceless boy for his cruelty, then a stronger man attcaks the man for his cruelty to the boy. Each believes the other to be unjust and cruel, and himself to be just and humane; and doubtless most of all would the boy justify his conduct toward the animal as altogether necessary. Thus does ignorance keep alive hatred and strife; thus do men blindly inflict suffering upon themselves, living in passion and resentment, and not finding the true way in life. Hatred is met with hatred, passion with passion, strife with strife. The man who kills is himself killed; the thief who lives by depriving others is himself deprived; the beast that preys on others is hunted and killed; the accuser is accused, the condemner is condemned, the denouncer is persecuted.

> "By this the slayer's knife doth stab himself,
> The unjust judge has lost his own defender,
> The false tongue dooms its lie, the creeping thief
> And spoiler rob to render.
> Such is the Law."

Passion, also has its active and passive sides. Fool and fraud, oppressor and slave, aggressor and retaliator, the charlatan and the superstitious, complement each other, and come together by the operation of the Law of Justice. Men unconsciously cooperate in the mutual production of affliction; "the blind lead the blind, and both fall together into the ditch." Pain, grief, sorrow, and misery are the fruits of which passion is the flower.

Where the passion-bound soul sees only injustice, the good man, he who has conquered passion, sees cause and effect, sees the Supreme Justice. It is impossible for such a man to regard himself as treated unjustly, because he has ceased to see injustice. He knows that no one can injure or cheat him, having ceased to injure or cheat himself. However passionately or ignorantly men may act towards him, it cannot possibly cause him any pain, for he knows that whatever comes to him (it may be abuse and persecution) can only come as the effect of what he himself has formerly sent out. He therefore regards all things as good, rejoices in all things, loves his enemies and blesses them that curse him, regarding them as the blind but beneficent instruments by which he is enabled to pay his moral debts to the Great Law.

The good man, having put away all resentment, retaliation, self-seeking, and egotism, has arrived at a state of equilibrium,and has thereby become identified with the Eternal and Universal Equilibrium. Having lifted himself above the blind forces of passion, he understands those forces, contemplates them with a calm penetrating insight, like the solitary dweller upon a mountain who looks down upon the conflict of the storms beneath his feet. For him, injustice has ceased, and he sees ignorance and suffering on the one hand and enlightenment and bliss on the other. He sees that not only do the fool and the slave need his sympathy, but that the fraud and the oppressor are equally in need of it, and so his compassion is extended towards all.

The Supreme Justice and the Supreme Love are one. Cause and effect cannot be avoided; consequences cannot be escaped.

While a man is given to hatred, resentment, anger and condemnation, he is subject to injustice as the dreamer to his dream, and cannot do otherwise than see injustice; but he who has overcome those fiery and binding elements, knows that unerring Justice presides over all, that in reality there is no such thing as injustice in the whole of the universe.

The Use Of Reason

We have heard it said that reason is a blind guide, and that it draws men away from Truth rather than leads them to it. If this were true, it were better to remain, or to become, unreasonable, and to persuade others so to do. We have found, however, that the diligent cultivation of the divine faculty of reason brings about calmness and mental poise, and enables one to meet cheerfully the problems and difficulties of life.

It is true there is a higher light than reason; even that of the Spirit of Truth itself, but without the aid of reason, Truth cannot be apprehended. They who refuse to trim the lamp of reason will never, whilst they so refuse, perceive the light of Truth, for the light of reason is a reflection of that Light.

Reason is a purely abstract quality, and comes midway between the animal and divine consciousness in man, and leads, if rightly employed, from the darkness of one to the Light of the other. It is true that reason may be enlisted in the service of the lower, self-seeking nature, but this is only a result of its partial and imperfect exercise. A fuller development of reason leads away from the selfish nature, and ultimately allies the soul with the highest, the divine.

That spiritual perceival who, searching for the Holy Grail of the Perfect Life, is again and again

> "left alone,
> And wearying in a land of sand and thorns,"

is not so stranded because he has followed reason, but because he is still clinging to, and is reluctant to leave, some remnants of his lower nature. He who will use the light of reason as a torch to search for Truth will not be left at last in comfortless darkness.

"Come, now, and let us reason together, saith the Lord; though your sins be as scarlet, they shall be as white as snow."

Many men and women pass through untold sufferings, and at last die in their sins, because they refuse to reason; because they cling to those dark delusions which even a faint glimmer of the light of reason would dispel; and all must use their reason freely, fully, and faithfully, who would exchange the scarlet robe of sin and suffering for the white garment of blamelessness and peace.

It is because we have proved and know these truths that we exhort men to

> "tread the middle road, whose course
> Bright reason traces, and soft quiet
> smooths,"

for reason leads away from passion and selfishness into the quiet ways of sweet persuasion and gentle forgiveness, and he will never be led astray, nor will he follow blind guides, who faithfully adheres to the Apostolic injunction, "Prove all things, and hold fast that which is good." They, therefore, who despise the light of reason, despise the Light of Truth.

Large numbers of people are possessed of the strange delusion that reason is somehow intimately connected with the denial of the existence of God. This is probably due to the fact that those who try to prove that there is no God usually profess to take their stand upon reason, while those who try to prove the reverse generally profess to take their stand on faith. Such argumentative combatants, however, are frequently governed more by prejudice than either reason or faith, their object being not to find Truth, but to defend and confirm a preconceived opinion.

Reason is concerned, not with ephemeral opinions, but with the established truth of things, and he who is possessed of the faculty of reason in its purity and excellence can never be enslaved by prejudice, and will put from him all preconceived opinions as worthless. He will neither attempt to prove nor disprove, but after balancing extremes and bringing together all apparent contradictions, he will carefully and dispassionately weigh and consider them, and so arrive at Truth.

Reason is, in reality, associated with all that is pure and gentle, moderate and just. It is said of a violent man that he is "unreasonable," of a kind and considerate man that he is "reasonable," and of an insane man that he has "lost his reason." Thus it is seen that the word is used, even to a great extent unconsciously, though none the less truly, in a very comprehensive sense, and though reason is not actually love and thoughtfulness and gentleness and sanity, it leads to and is intimately connected with these divine qualities, and cannot, except for purposes of analysis, be dissociated from them.

Reason represents all that is high and noble in man. It distinguishes him from the brute which blindly follows its animal inclinations, and just in the degree that man disobeys the voice of reason and follows his inclinations does he become brutish. As Milton says:

Reason in man obscured, or not obeyed.

And upstart passions catch the government
From reason, and to servitude reduce
Man till then free."

The following definition of "reason" from Nuttall's Dictionary will give some idea of the comprehensiveness of the word:

The cause, ground, principle, or motive of anything said or done; efficient cause; final cause; the faculty of intelligence in man; especially the faculty by which we arrive at necessary truth. It will thus be seen that "reason" is a term, the breadth of which is almost sufficient to embrace even Truth itself, and Archbishop Trench tells us in his celebrated work On the Study of Words that the terms Reason and Word "are indeed so essentially one and the same that the Greek language has one word for them both," so that the Word of God is the Reason of God; and one of the renderings of Lao-tze's "Tao" is Reason, so that in the chinese translation of our New Testament, St.John's Gospel runs; "In the beginning was the Tao."

To the undeveloped and uncharitable mind all words have narrow applications, but as a man enlarges his sympathies and broadens his intelligence, words become filled with rich meanings and assume comprehensive proportions. Let us therefore cease from foolish quarrelings about words, and, like reasonable beings, search for principles and practise those things which make for unity and peace.

Self-Discipline

A man does not live until he begins to discipline himself; he merely exists. Like an animal he gratifies his desires and pursues his inclinations just where they may lead him. He is happy as a beast is happy, because he is not conscious of what he is depriving himself; he suffers as the beast suffers, because he does not know the way out of suffering. He does not intelligently reflect upon life, and lives in a series of sensations, longings, and confused memories which are unrelated to any central idea or principle. A man whose inner life is so ungoverned and chaotic must necessarily manifest this confusion in the visible conditions of his outer life in the world; and though for a time, running with the stream of his desires, he may draw to himself a more or less large share of the outer necessities and comforts of life, he never achieves any real success nor accomplishes any real good, and sooner or later wordly failure and disaster are inevitable, as the direct result of the inward failure to properly adjust and regulate those mental forces which make the outer life.

Before a man accomplish anything of an enduring nature in the world he must first of all acquire some measure of success in the management of his own mind. This is as mathematical a truism as that two and two are four, for, "out of the heart are the issues of life." If a man cannot govern the forces within himself, he cannot hold a firm hand upon the outer activities which form his visible life. On the other hand, as a man succeeds, in governing himself he rises to higher and higher levels of power and usefulness and success in the world.

The only difference between the life of the beast and that of the undisciplined man is that the man has a wider variety of desires, and experiences a greater intensity of suffering. It may be said of such a man that he is dead, being truly dead to self-control, chastity, fortitude, and all the nobler qualities which constitute life. In the consciousness of such a man the crucified Christ lies entombed, awaiting that resurrection which shall revivify the mortal sufferer, and wake him up to a knowledge of tha realities of his existence.

With the practice of self-discipline a man begins to live, for he then commences to rise above the inward confusion and to adjust his conduct to a steadfast centre within himself. He ceases to follow where inclination leads him, reins in the steed of his desires, and lives in accordance with the dictates of reason and wisdom. Hitherto his life has been without purpose or meaning, but now he begins to consciously mould his own destiny; he is "clothed and in his right mind."

In the process of self-discipline there are three stages namely;

Relinquishment

A man begins to discipline himself by controlling those passions which have hitherto controlled him; he resists temptation and guards himself against all those tendencies to selfish gratifications which are so easy and natural, and which have formerly dominated him. He brings his appetite into subjection, and begins to eat as a reasonable and responsible being, practising moderation and thoughtfulness in the selection of his food, with the object of making his body a pure instrument through which he may live and act as becomes a man, and no longer degarding that body by pandering to gustatory pleasure. He puts a check upon his tongue, his temper, and, in fact, his every animal desire and tendency, and this he does by referring all his acts to a fixed centre within himself. It is a process of living from within outward, instead of, as formerly, from without inward. He conceives of an ideal, and, enshrining that ideal in the sacred recesses of his heart, he regulates his conduct in accordance with its exaction and demands.

There is a philosophical hypothesis that at the heart of every atom and every aggregation of atoms in the universe there is a motionless center which is the sustaining source of all the universal activities. Be this as it may, there is certainly in the heart of every man and woman a selfless centre without which the outer man could not be, and the ignoring of which leads to suffering and confusion. This selfless center which takes the form, in the mind, of an ideal of unselfishness and spotless purity, the attainment of which is desirable, is man's eternal refuge from the storms of passion and all the conflicting elements of his lower nature. It is the Rock of Ages, the Christ within, the divine and immortal in all men.

As a man practises self-control he approximates more and more to this inward reality, and is less and less swayed by passion and grief, pleasure and pain, and lives a steadfast and virtuous life, manifesting manly strength and fortitude. The restraining of the passions, however, is merely the initial stage in self-discipline, and is immediately followed by the process of Purification. By this a man so purifies himself as to take passion out of the heart and mind altogether; not merely restraining it when it rises within him, but preventing it from rising altogether. By merely restraining his passions a man can never arrive at peace, can never actualise his ideal; he must purify those passions.

It is in the purification of his lower nature that a man becomes strong and god-like, standing firmly upon the ideal centre within, and rendering all temptations powerless and ineffectual. This purification is effected by thoughtful care, earnest meditation, and holy aspiration; and as success is achieved confusion of mind and life pass away, and calmness of mind and spiritualized conduct ensure.

True strength and power and usefulness are born of self-purification, for the lower animal forces are not lost, but are transmuted into intellectual and spiritual energy. The pure life (Pure in thought and deed) is a life of conservation of energy; the impure life (even should the impurity not extent beyond thought) is a life of dissipation of energy. The pure man is more capable, and therefore more fit to succeed in his plans and to accomplish his purposes than the impure. Where the impure man fails, the pure man will step in and be victorious, because he directs his energies with a calmer mind and a greater definiteness and strength of purpose.

With the growth in purity; all the elements which constitute a strong and virtuous manhood are developed in an increasing degree of power, and as a man brings his lower nature into subjection, and makes his passions do his bidding, just so much will he mould the outer circumstances of his life, and influence others for good.

The third stage of self-discipline, that of Relinquishment, is a process of letting the lower desires and all impure and unworthy thoughts drop out of the mind, and also refusing to give them any admittance, leaving them to perish. As a man grows purer, he perceives that all evil is powerless, unless it receives his encouragement, and so he ignores it, and lets it pass out of his life. It is by pursuing this aspect of self-discipline that a man enters into and realises the divine life, and manifests those qualities which are distinctly divine, such as wisdom, patience, non-resistance, compassion, and love. It is here, also, where a man becomes consciously immortal, rising above all the fluctuations and uncertainties of life, and living in and intelligent and unchangeable peace.

By self-discipline a man attains to every degree of virtue and holiness, and finally becomes a purified son of God, realising his oneness with the central heart of all things.

Without self-discipline a man drifts lower and lower, approximating more and more nearly to the beast, until at last he grovels, a lost creature, in the mire of his own befoulment. By self-discipline a man rises higher and higher, approximating more and more nearly to the divine, until at last he stands erect in his divine dignity, a saved soul, glorified by the radiance of his purity. Let a man discipline himself, and he will live; let a man cease to discipline himself, and he will perish. As a tree grows in beauty, health, and fruitfulness by being carefully pruned and tended, so a man grows in grace and beauty of life by cutting away all the branches of evil from his mind, and as he tends and develops the good by constant and unfailing effort.

As a man by practice acquires proficiency in his craft, so the earnest man acquires proficiency in goodness and wisdom. Men shrink from self-discipline because in its early stages it is painful and repellent, and the yielding to desire is, at first, sweet and inviting; but the end of desire is darkness and unrest, whereas the fruits of discipline are immortality and peace.

Resolution

Resolution is the directing and impelling force in individual progress. Without it no substantial work can be accomplished. Not until a man brings resolution to bear upon his life does he consciously and rapidly develop, for a life without resolution is a life without aims, and a life without aims is a drifting and unstable thing.

Resolution may of course be linked to downward tendencies, but it is more usually the companion of noble aims and lofty ideals, and Iam dealing with it in this its highest use and application.

When a man makes a resolution, it means that he is dissatisfied with his condition, and is commencing to take himself in hand with a view to producing a better piece of workmanship out of the mental materials of which his character and life are composed, and in so far as he is true to his resolution he will succeed in accomplishing his purpose.

The vows of the saintly once are holy resolutions directed toward some victory over self, and the beautiful achievements of holy men and the glorious conquests of the Divine Teachers were rendered possible and actual by the pursuit of unswerving resolution.

To arrive at the fixed determination to walk a higher path than heretofore, although it reveals the great difficulties which have to be surmounted, it yet makes possible the treading of that path, and illuminates its dark places with the golden halo of success.

The true resolution is the crisis of long thought, protracted struggle, or fervent but unsatisfied aspiration. It is no light thing, no whimsical impulse or vague desire, but a solemn and irrevocable determination not to rest nor cease from effort until the high purpose which is held in view is fully accomplished.

Half-hearted and premature resolution is no resolution at all, and is shattered at the first difficulty.

A man should be slow to form a resolution. He should searchingly examine his position and take into consideration every circumstance and difficulty connected with his decision, and should be fully prepared to meet them. He should be sure that he completely understands the nature of his resolution, that his mind is finally made up, and that he is without fear and doubt in the matter. With the mind thus prepared, the resolution that is formed will not be departed from, and by the aid of it a man will, in due time, accomplish his strong purpose.

Hasty resolutions are futile.

The mind must be fortified to endure.

Immediately the resolution to walk a higher path is made, temptation and trial begin. Men have found that no sooner have they decided to lead a truer and nobler life than they have been overwhelmed with such a torrent of new temptations and difficulties as make their position almost unendurable, and many men, because of this, relinquish their resolution.

But these temptations and trials are a necessary part of the work of regeneration upon which the man has decided and must be hailed as friends and met with courage if the resolution is to do its work. For what is the real nature of a resolution? Is it not the sudden checking of a particular stream of conduct, and the endeavour to open up an entirely new channel? Think of an engineer who decides to turn the course of a powerfully running stream or river in another direction. He must first cut his new channel, and must take every precaution to avoid failure in the carrying out of his undertaking. But when he comes to the all-important task of directing the stream into its new channel, then the flowing force, which for ages has steadily pursued its accustomed course, becomes refractory, and all the patience and care and skill of the engineer will be required for the successful completion of the work. It is even so with the man who determines to turn his course of conduct in another and higher direction. Having prepared his mind, which is the cutting of a new channel, he then proceeds to the work of redirecting his mental forces - which have hitherto flowed on uninterruptedly - into the new course. Immediately this is attempted, the arrested energy begins to assert itself in the form of powerful temptations and trials hitherto unknown and unencountered. And this is exactly as it should be; it is the law; and the same law that is in the water is in the mind. No man can improve upon the established law of things, but he can learn to understand the law instead of complaining, and wishing things were different. The man who understands all that is involved in the regeneration of his mind will "glory in tribulations," knowing that only by passing through them can he gain strength, obtain purity of heart, and arrive at peace. And as the engineer at last (perhaps after many mistakes and failures) succeeds in getting the stream to flow on peacefully in the broader and better channel, and the turbulence of the water is spent, and all dams can be removed, so the man of resolution at last succeeds in directing his thoughts and acts into the better and nobler way to which he aspires, and temptations and trials give place to steadfast strength and settled peace.

He whose life is not in harmony with his conscience and who is anxious to remedy his mind and conduct in a particular direction, let him first mature his purpose by earnest thought and self-examination, and having arrived at a final conclusion, let him frame his resolution, and having done so let him not swerve from it, let him remain true to his decision under all circumstances, and he cannot fail to achieve his good purpose; for the Great Law ever shields and protects him who, no matter how deep his sins, or how great and many his failures and mistakes, has, deep in his heart, resolved upon the finding of a better way, and every obstacle must at last give way before a matured and unshaken resolution.

The Glorious Conquest

Truth can only be apprehended by the conquest of self.

Blessedness can only be arrived at by overcoming the lower nature.

The way of Truth is barred by a man's self.

The only enemies that can actually hinder him are his own passions and delusions.

Until a man realises this, and commences to cleanse his heart, he has not found the Path which leads to knowledge and peace.

Until passion is transcended, Truth remains unknown. This is the Divine Law.

A man cannot keep his passions and have Truth as well.

Error is not slain until selfishness is dead.

The overcoming of self is no mystical theory, but a very real and practical thing.

It is a process which must be pursued daily and hourly, with unswerving faith and undaunted resolution if any measure of success is to be achieved.

The process is one of orderly growth, having its sequential stages, like the growth of a tree; and as fruit can only be produced by carefully and patiently training the tree even so the pure and satisfying fruits of holiness can only be obtained by faithfully and patiently training the mind in the growth of right thought and conduct.

There are five steps in the overcoming of passion (which includes all bad habits and particular forms of wrong-doing) which I will call:

Victory

When men fail to overcome their sins, it is because they try to begin at the wrong end. They want to have the stage of Victory without passing through the previous four stages. They are in the position of a gardener who wants to produce good fruit without training and attending to his trees.

Repression consists in checking and controlling the wrong act (such as an outburst of temper, a hasty or unkind word, a selfish indulgence etc.), and not allowing it to take actual form. This is equivalent to the gardener nipping off the useless buds and branches from his tree. It is a necessary process, but a painful one. The tree bleeds while undergoing the process, and the gardener knows that it must not be taxed too severely. The heart also bleeds when it refuses to return passion for passion, whan it ceases to defend and justify itself. It is the process of "mortifying the members" of which St. Paul speaks.

But this repression is only the beginning of self-conquest. When it is made an end in itself, and there is no object of finally purifying the heart, that is a stage of hypocrisy; a hiding of one's true nature, and striving to appear better in the eyes of others than one really is. In that case it is an evil, but when adopted as the first stage toward complete purification, it is good. Its practice leads to the second stage of Endurance, or forbearance, in which one silently endures the pain which arises in the mind when it is brought in contact with certain actions and attitudes of other minds toward one. As success is attained in this stage, the striver comes to see that all his pain actually arises in his own weaknesses, and not in the wrong attitudes of others toward him, these latter being merely the means by which his sins are brought to the surface and revealed to him. He thus gradually exonerates all others from blame in his falls and lapses of conduct, and accuses only himself, and so learns to love those who thus unconsciously reveal to him his sins and shortcomings.

Having passed through these two stages of self-crucifixion, the disciple enters the third, that of Elimination, in which the wrong thought which lay behind the wrong act is cast from the mind immediately it appears. At this stage, conscious strength and holy joy begin to take the place of pain, and the mind having become comparatively calm, the striver is enabled to gain a deeper insight into the complexities of his mind, and thus to understand the inception, growth, and outworking of sin. This is the stage of Understanding.

Perfection in understanding leads to the final conquest of self, a conquest so complete that the sin can no more rise in the mind even as a thought or impression; for when the knowledge of sin is complete; when it is known in its totality, from its inception as a seed in the mind to its ripened outgrowth as act and consequence, then it can no more be allowed a place in life, but it is abandoned for ever. Then the mind is at peace. The wrong acts of others no longer arouse wrong and pain in the mind of the disciple. He is glad and calm and wise. He is filled with Love, and blessedness abides with him. And this is Victory!

Contentment In Activity

The confounding of a positive spiritual virtue or principle with a negative animal vice is common amongst writers even of what is called the "Advance Thought School," and much valuable energy is frequently expended in criticising and condemning, where a little calm reasoning would have revealed a greater light, and led to the exercise of a broader charity.

The other day I came across a vigorous attack upon the teaching of "Love," wherein the writer condemned such teaching as weakly, foolish, and hypocritical. Needless to say, that which he was condemning as "Love," was merely weak sentimentality and hypocrisy.

Another writer in condemning "meekness" does not know that what he calls meekness is only cowardice, while another who attacks "chastity" as "a snare," is really confusing painful and hypocritical restraint with the virtue of chastity. And just lately I received a long letter from a correspondent who took great pains to show me that "contentment" is a vice, and is the source of innumerable evils.

That which my correspondent called "contentment" is, of course animal indifference. The spirit of indifference is incompatible with progress, whereas the spirit of contentment may, and does, attend the highest form of activity, the truest advancement and development. Indolence is the twin sister of indifference, but cheerful and ready action is the friend of contentment.

Contentment is a virtue which becomes lofty and spiritual in its later developments, as the mind is trained to perceive and the heart to receive the guidance, in all things, of a merciful law.

To be contented does not mean to forego effort; it means to free effort from anxiety; it does not mean to be satisfied with sin and ignorance and folly, but to rest happily in duty done, work acomplished.

A man may be said to be content to lead a grovelling life, to remain in sin and in debt, but such a man's true state is one of indifference to his duty, his obligations, and the just claims of his fellow-men. He cannot truly be said to possess the virtue of contentment; he does not experience the pure and abiding joy which is the accompaniment of active contentment; so far as his true nature is concerned he is a sleeping soul, and sooner or later will be awakened by intense suffering, having passed through which he will find that true contentment which is the outcome of honest effort and true living.

There are three things with which a man should be content:

With whatever happens.

With his friendships and possessions.

With his pure thoughts.

Contented with whatever happens, he will escape grief; with his friends and possessions, he will avoid anxiety and wretchedness; and with his pure thoughts, he will never go back to suffer and grovel in impurities.

There are three things with which a man should not be content:

With his opinions.

With his character.

With his spiritual condition.

Not content with his opinions, he will continually increase in intelligence; not content with his character, he will ceaselessly grow in strength and virtue; and not content with his spiritual condition, he will, everyday, enter into a larger wisdom and fuller blessedness. In a word, a man should be contented, but not indifferent to his development as a responsible and spiritual being.

The truly contented man works energetically and faithfully, and accepts all results with an untroubled spirit, trusting, at first, that all is well, but afterwards, with the growth of enlightenment, knowing that results exactly correspond with efforts. Whatsoever material possessions come to him, come not by greed and anxiety and strife, but by right thought, wise action, and pure exertion.

The Temple of Brotherhood

Universal Brotherhood is the supreme Ideal of Humanity, and towards that Ideal the world is slowly but surely moving.

Today, as never before, numbers of earnest men and women are striving to make this Ideal tangible and real; Fraternities are springing up on every hand, and Press and Pulpit, the world over, are preaching the Brotherhood of Man.

The unselfish elements in all such efforts cannot fail to have their effect upon the race, and are with certainty urging it towards the goal of its noblest aspirations; but the ideal state has not yet manifested through any outward organisation, and societies formed for the purpose of propagating Brotherhood are continually being shattered to pieces by internal dissension.

The Brotherhood for which Humanity sighs is withheld from actuality by Humanity itself; nay, more, it is frustrated even by men who work zealously for it is a desirable possibility; and this because the purely spiritual nature of Brotherhood is not perceived, and the principles involved, as well as the individual course of conduct necessary to perfect unity, are not comprehended.

Brotherhood as a human organisation cannot exist so long as any degree of self-seeking reigns in the hearts of men and women who band themselves together for any purpose, as such self-seeking must eventually rend the Seamless Coat of loving unity. But although organised Brotherhood has so far largely failed, any man may realise Brotherhood in its perfection, and know it in all its beauty and completion, if he will make himself of a wise, pure, and loving spirit, removing from his mind every element of strife, and learning to practise those divine qualities without which Brotherhood is but a mere theory, opinion, or illusive dream.

For Brotherhood is at first spiritual, and its outer manifestation in the world must follow as a natural sequence.

As a spiritual reality it must be discovered by each man for himself, and in the only place where spiritual realities can be found - within himself, and it rests with each whether he shall choose or refuse it.

There are four chief tendencies in the human mind which are destructive of Brotherhood, and which bar the way to its comprehension, namely:

Condemnation

Where these are there can be no Brotherhood; in whatsoever heart these hold sway, discord rules, and Brotherhood is not realised, for these tendencies are, in their very nature, dark and selfish amd always make for disruption and destruction. From these four things proceeds that serpent brood of false actions and conditions which poison the heart of man, and fill the world with suffering and sorrow.

Out of the spirit of pride proceed envy, resentment, and opinionativeness. Pride envies the position, influence, or goodness of others; it thinks, "Iam more deserving than this man or this woman"; it also continually finds occasion for resenting the actions of others, and says, "I have been snubbed," "I have been insulted," and thinking altogether of his own excellence, it sees no excellence in others.

From the spirit of self-love proceed egotism, lust for power, and disparagement and contempt. Self-love worships the personality in which it moves; it is lost in the adoration and glorification of that "I", that "self" which has no real existence, but is a dark dream and a delusion. It desires pre-eminence over others, and thinks, "Iam great," "Iam more important than others"; it also disparages others, and bestows upon them contempt, seeing no beauty in them, being lost in the contemplation of its own beauty.

From the spirit of hatred proceed slander, cruelty, reviling, and anger. It strives to overcome evil by adding evil to it. It says, "This man has spoken of me ill, I will speak still more ill of him and thus teach him a lesson." It mistakes cruelty for kindness, and causes its possessor to revile a reproving friend. It feeds the flames of anger with bitter and rebellious thoughts.

From the spirit of condemnation proceed accusation, false pity, and false judgement. It feeds itself on the contemplation of evil, and cannot see the good. It has eyes for evil only, and finds it in almost every thing and every person. It sets up an arbitrary standard of right and wrong by which to judge others, and it thinks, "This man does not do as I would have him do, he is therefore evil, and I will denounce him." So blind is the spirit of condemnation that whilst rendering its possessor incapable of judging himself, it causes him to set himself up as the judge of all the earth.

From the four tendencies enumerated, no element of brotherliness can proceed. They are deadly mental poisons, and he who allows them to rankle in his mind, cannot apprehend the peaceful principles on which Brotherhood rests.

Then there are chiefly four divine qualities which are productive of Brotherhood; which are, as it were, the foundation stones on which it rests, namely:

Pleasant Pastures Of Peace

He who aspires to the bettering of himself and humanity should ceaselessly strive to arrive at the exercise of that blessed attitude of mind by which he is enabled to put himself, mentally and sympathetically in the place of others, and so, instead of harshly and falsely judging them, and thereby making himself unhappy without adding to the happiness of those others, he will enter into their experience, will understand their particular frame of mind, and will feel for them and sympathise with them.

One of the great obstacles to the attainment of such an attitude of mind is, prejudice, and until this is removed it is impossible to act toward others as we would wish others to act toward us.

Prejudice is destructive of kindness, sympathy, love and true judgment, and the strength of a man's prejudice will be the measure of his harshness and unkindness toward others, for prejudice and cruelty are inseparable.

There is no rationality in prejudice, and, immediately it is aroused in a man he ceases to act as a reasonable being, and gives way to rashness, anger, and injurious excitement. He does not consider his words nor regard the feelings and liberties of those against whom his prejudices are directed. He has, for the time being, forfeited his manhood, and has descended to the level of an irrational creature.

While a man is determined to cling to his preconceived opinions, mistaking them for Truth, and refuses to consider dispassionately the position of others, he cannot escape hatred nor arrive at blessedness.

The man who strives after gentleness, who aspires to act unselfishly toward others, will put away all his passionate prejudice and petty opinions, and will gradually acquire the power of thinking and feeling for others, of understanding their particular state of ignorance or knowledge, and thereby entering fully into their hearts and lives, sympathizing with them and seeing them as they are.

Such a man will not oppose himself to the prejudices of others by introducing his own, but will seek to allay prejudice by introducing sympathy and love, striving to bring out all that is good in men, encouraging the good by appealing to it, and discouraging the evil by ignoring it. He will realise the good in the unselfish efforts of others, though their outward methods may be very different from his own, and will so rid his heart of hatred, and will fit it with love and blessedness.

When a man is prone to harshly judge and condemn others, he should inquire how far he falls short himself; he should also reconsider those periods of suffering when he himself was misjudged and misunderstood, and, gathering wisdom and love from his own bitter experience, should studiously and self-sacrificingly refrain from piercing with anguish hearts that are as yet too weak to ignore, too immature and uninstructed to understand.

Sympathy is not required towards those who are purer and more enlightened than one's self, as the purer one lives above the necessity for it. In such a case reverence should be exercised, with a striving to lift one's self upto the purer level, and so enter into possession of the larger life. Nor can a man fully understand one who is wiser than himself, and before condemning, he should earnestly ask himself whether he is, after all, better than the man whom he has singled out as the object of his bitterness. If he is, let him bestow sympathy. If he is not, let him exercise reverence.

For thousands of years the sages have taught, both by precept and example, that evil is only overcome by good, yet still that lesson for the majority, remains unlearned. It is a lesson profound in its simplicity, and difficult to learn because men are blinded by the illusions of self. Men are still engaged in resenting, condemning, and fighting the evil in their own fellow-men, thereby increasing the delusion in their own hearts, and adding to the world's sum of misery and suffering. When they find out that their own resentment must be eradicated, and love put in its place, evil will perish for lack of sustenance.

> "With burning brain and heart of hate,
> I sought my wronger, early, late,
> And all the wretched night and day
> My dream and thought was slay, and slay.
> My better self rose uppermost,
> The beast within my bosom lost
> Itself in love; peace from afar
> Shone o'er me radiant like a star.
> I Slew my wronger with a deed,
> A deed of love; I made him bleed
> With kindness, and I filled for years
> His soul with tenderness and tears."

Dislike, resentment, and condemnation are all forms of hatred, and evil cannot cease until these are taken out of the heart.

But the obliterating of injuries from the mind is merely one of the beginnings in wisdom. There is a still higher and better way. And that way is so to purify the heart and enlighten the mind that, far from having to forget injuries, there will be none to remember. For it is only pride and self that can be injured and wounded by the actions and attitudes of others; and he who takes pride and self out of his heart can never think the thought, "I have been injured by another" or "I have been wronged by another."

From a purified heart proceeds the right comprehension of things; and from the right comprehension of things proceeds the life that is peaceful, freed from bitterness and suffering, calm and wise. He who thinks, "This man has injured me," has not perceived the Truth in life; falls short of that enlightenment which disperses the erroneous idea of evil as a thing to be hatefully resented. He who is troubled and disturbed about the sins of others is far from Truth; he who is troubled and disturbed about his own sins is very near to the Gate of Wisdom. He in whose heart the flames of resentment burn, cannot know Peace nor understand Truth; he who will banish resentment from his heart, will know and understand.

He who has taken evil out of his own heart cannot resent or resist it in others, for he is enlightened as to its origin and nature, and knows it as a manifestation of the mistakes of ignorance. With the increase of enlightenment, sin becomes impossible. He who sins, does not understand; he who understands does not sin.

The pure man maintains his tenderness of his heart toward those who ignorantly imagine they can do him harm. The wrong attitude of others toward him does not trouble him; his heart is at rest in Compassion and Love.

Blessed is he who has no wrongs to remember, no injuries to forget; in whose pure heart no hateful thought about another can take root and flourish.

Let those who aim at the right life, who believe that they love Truth, cease to passionately oppose themselves to others, and let them strive to calmly and wisely understand them, and in thus acting toward others they will be conquering themselves; and while sympathizing with others, their own souls will be fed with the heavenly dews of kindness, and their hearts be strengthened and refreshed in the *Pleasant Pastures of Peace.*